TINY TERRORS
BACTERIA

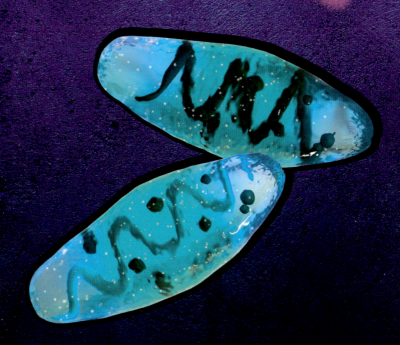

JILL KEPPELER

PowerKiDS press

Published in 2024 by The Rosen Publishing Group, Inc.
2544 Clinton Street, Buffalo, NY 14224

Copyright © 2024 by The Rosen Publishing Group, Inc.

All rights reserved. No part of this book may be reproduced in any form without permission in writing from the publisher, except by a reviewer.

Portions of this work were originally authored by Greg Roza and published as *Deadly Bacteria*. All new material in this edition was authored by Jill Keppeler.

Editor: Dwayne Hicks
Book Design: Michael Flynn

Photo Credits: Cover sokolova_sv/Shutterstock.com; (series background) Ruswantodarkness/Shutterstock.com; pp. 5, 13 Kateryna Kon/Shutterstock.com; p. 7 FrentaN/Shutterstock.com; p. 9 https://commons.wikimedia.org/wiki/File:Anthonie_van_Leeuwenhoek_(1632-1723)._Natuurkundige_te_Delft_Rijksmuseum_SK-A-957.jpeg; p. 10 Mikhail Sedov/Shutterstock.com; p. 11 Yayah_Ai/Shutterstock.com; p. 15 Yulia YasPe/Shutterstock.com; p. 17 AJP/Shutterstock.com; p. 18 maimoon/Shutterstock.com; p. 19 https://commons.wikimedia.org/wiki/File:John_Snow.jpg; p. 21 Prostock-studio/Shutterstock.com.

Cataloging-in-Publication Data

Names: Keppeler, Jill.
Title: Bacteria / Jill Keppeler
Description: New York : Powerkids Press, 2024. | Series: Tiny terrors | Includes index, glossary, and bibliographic information
Identifiers: ISBN 9781642826180 (pbk) | ISBN 9781642826197 (library bound) | ISBN 9781642826203 (ebook)
Subjects: LCSH: Bacteria– Juvenile literature | Microbiology–Juvenile literature
Classification: LCC QR74.8 K47 2023 | DDC 579.3–dc24

Manufactured in the United States of America

Some of the images in this book illustrate individuals who are models. The depictions do not imply actual situations or events.

CPSIA Compliance Information: Batch #CSPK24. For Further Information contact Rosen Publishing at 1-800-237-9932.

CONTENTS

THE TINIEST TERROR 4
SO MANY BACTERIA 6
FATHER OF MICROBIOLOGY 8
TINY TROUBLEMAKERS 10
THE BLACK DEATH 12
E. COLI & CO. 14
TB TERRORS 16
THE BLUE DEATH 18
FIGHTING BACK 20
GLOSSARY 22
FOR MORE INFORMATION 23
INDEX 24

THE TINIEST TERROR

What's the tiniest creature you can think of? A kitten? A mouse? Think smaller. A bumblebee? A fly? Bacteria are even smaller. These tiny organisms, or living things, are only one cell. We need a **microscope** if we want to see them.

Bacteria live almost everywhere. They live in our food and in the soil. They even live in and on our bodies! That might sound weird or icky, but some bacteria help us. However, some bacteria can make us very sick.

DEADLY DETAILS

A virus is different than a bacterium. (That means one bacteria.) A virus is smaller. It can't live without another cell.

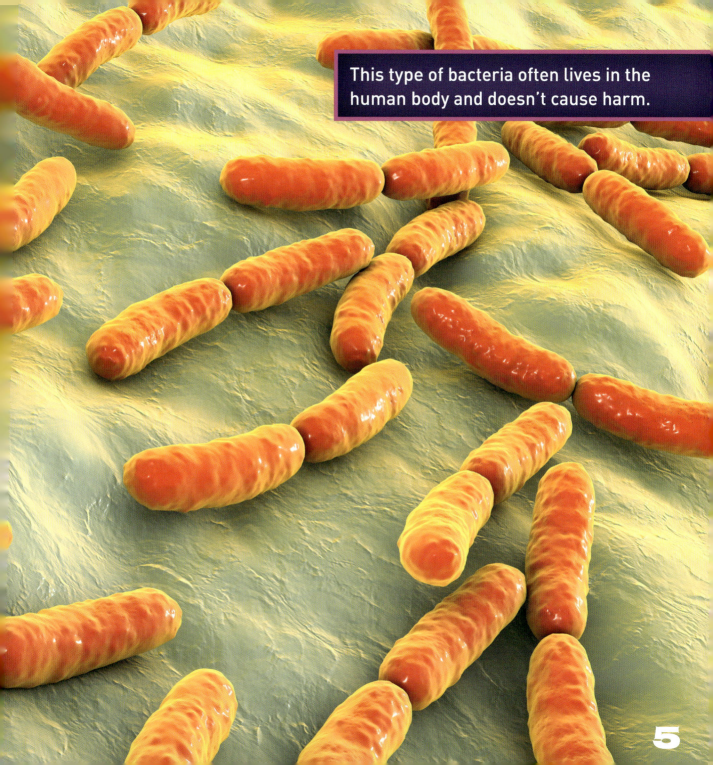
This type of bacteria often lives in the human body and doesn't cause harm.

SO MANY BACTERIA

There are thousands of kinds of bacteria. They're one of the oldest types of organisms on the planet. They've been here **billions** of years! They're very good at evolving, or growing and changing over time. They can have many different shapes.

A group, or colony, of bacteria can grow very fast. They make more of themselves by dividing, or splitting, in half again and again. In one day, one bacterium can become billions of bacteria.

DEADLY DETAILS

Cyanobacteria are a type of bacteria. They usually live in water and make their own food. They produce **oxygen**.

People have found bacteria fossils in very old rocks. In fact, the oldest known fossils are of cyanobacteria.

FATHER OF MICROBIOLOGY

For a long time, people had guessed that there were tiny creatures we couldn't see. Until the invention of the microscope, though, they couldn't know for sure. A Dutch scientist named Antonie van Leeuwenhoek (1632–1723) became interested in building microscopes. He was the first to see and describe, or tell about, bacteria through a microscope.

Leeuwenhoek is sometimes called the father of microbiology. This is the science dealing with microscopic forms of life. Because of this science, scientists learned about how some bacteria can cause illnesses.

Leeuwenhoek was mostly a self-taught scientist. He learned about science and microbiology all on his own.

TINY TROUBLEMAKERS

Bacteria can get into your body in many ways. You can breathe them in. They can also get in through cuts in your skin. Once they're safe and warm, the bacteria can **reproduce** and grow quickly. This can cause illness. Sometimes, it's harmful material, or matter, that bacteria create that causes disease, or illness.

DEADLY DETAILS

You can find *Salmonella* bacteria in many places, such as meats, fruits, and vegetables. You can also get these bacteria from animals. Always wash your hands after petting or holding an animal!

If you eat food that has harmful bacteria, it can make you sick. *Salmonella* bacteria are one kind of bacteria that may do this.

The human body's **immune system** will usually do its best to fight off harmful bacteria. Sometimes, though, it will need help from **vaccines** or **antibiotics**.

THE BLACK DEATH

A kind of bacteria called *Yersinia pestis* causes a disease called the plague. There are a few different forms of this disease. One form is the bubonic plague, which killed as much as one-third of Europe's population during the **Middle Ages**. This historic **pandemic** is called the Black Death.

The *Yersinia pestis* bacteria live in fleas that often live on rats or mice. It's likely that the Black Death spread because of black rats that traveled on sailing ships and along other trade routes, or paths.

DEADLY DETAILS

The Black Death spread very quickly, as much as a mile a day. The plague is a zoonosis, an illness that passes from animals to humans.

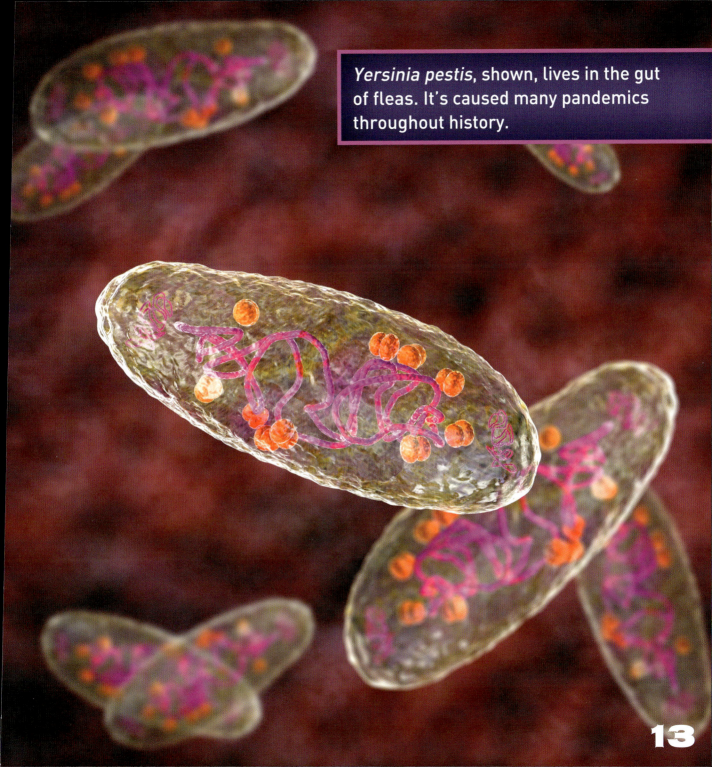

Yersinia pestis, shown, lives in the gut of fleas. It's caused many pandemics throughout history.

E. COLI & CO.

Plague isn't common, and today it can be treated. However, there are many common types of bacteria that can cause illness. You've probably heard of *Escherichia coli*—called *E. coli*. This is a kind of bacteria that lives in the stomach and **intestines** of humans and other animals.

Like *Salmonella, E. coli* can cause illness called food poisoning. There are a few kinds of *E. coli* that can cause very serious illness. They can even cause death.

DEADLY DETAILS

Having food poisoning caused by *E. coli* isn't fun. It can be pretty awful! But most people will get over it quickly on their own.

The best way to avoid food poisoning from *E. coli* is to always wash your hands after using the bathroom. Also, make sure to always cook food to the right temperature, or heat level.

TB TERRORS

The plague is scary and food poisoning caused by *E. coli* is more common, but tuberculosis, or TB, has killed more than 1 billion people over the years. This illness is caused by bacteria and usually involves the lungs. At one point, it was the leading killer in the United States and other parts of the world.

Even though we can now prevent and treat tuberculosis, many people worldwide still get it and die from it. In fact, it's one of the top 10 causes of death in the world.

DEADLY DETAILS

Tuberculosis can be treated with antibiotics. However, some forms of TB can resist, or fight, some drugs.

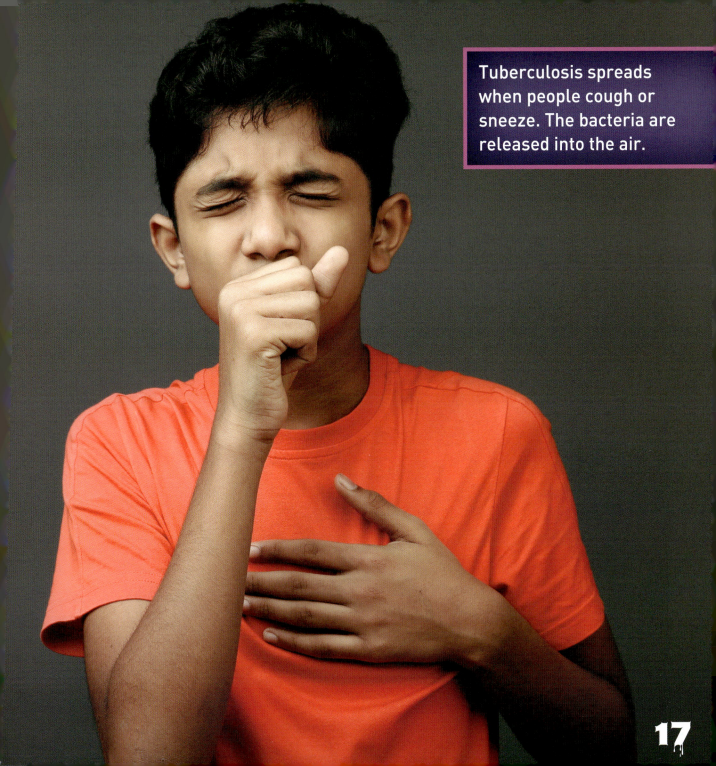
Tuberculosis spreads when people cough or sneeze. The bacteria are released into the air.

THE BLUE DEATH

Cholera is another bacterial disease that still causes deaths around the world. It can be treated, but it's almost always deadly if it isn't. It's particularly deadly to children. This **infection** of the intestines happens when someone eats or drinks food or water with the bacteria *Vibro cholerae*.

DEADLY DETAILS

Sometimes people call cholera the "blue death" because it can cause someone's skin to turn blue-gray due to lack of fluids, or liquids.

Vibro cholerae

British doctor John Snow studied a cholera outbreak in London in 1849. He figured out it spread through water. Still, many people didn't believe this for a long time.

Cholera has caused at least seven pandemics over the past 200 or so years. Its symptoms, or signs, include fever, stomach pain, throwing up, and **diarrhea**. Someone who has cholera can lose a lot of water quickly.

FIGHTING BACK

Bacteria make us sick, but we can fight back and stay safe. Stay away from people who are sick. Stay home yourself if you're sick. Wash your hands as much as you can, especially after using the bathroom and before or after touching food. Cover your mouth if you cough or sneeze. (And use your arm or elbow instead of your hands so you don't spread bacteria more.)

It's also very important to get vaccines for diseases when you can. This helps keep you and other people safe!

Tetanus is a disease caused by a bacterium. Many kids will get a vaccine for tetanus regularly.

GLOSSARY

antibiotic: A drug that can kill harmful bacteria in the body.

billion: A number equal to 1,000 million, or 1,000,000,000.

diarrhea: Very soft or runny solid waste from a person or animal, can be a sign of illness.

immune system: Parts of the body that fight germs and keep it healthy.

infection: An illness caused by germs entering the body.

intestine: A tubelike part in the body that helps digest food.

microscope: An instrument used for viewing very small objects.

Middle Ages: A time in European history from about AD 500 to 1500.

oxygen: A colorless, odorless gas that many animals, including people, need to breathe.

pandemic: A time or event in which a disease spreads quickly and affects many people in a wide area or around the world.

reproduce: When an animal creates another creature like itself.

vaccine: A shot that helps keep someone safe from an illness.

FOR MORE INFORMATION

BOOKS

Liu, Katrina. *How Do Vaccines Work?* San Francisco, CA: Lychee Press, 2022.

Mould, Steve. *The Bacteria Book: The Big World of Really Tiny Microbes.* New York, NY: DK Children, 2023.

Kroe, Kathryn. *What Are Bacteria?* Buffalo, NY: Cavendish Square, 2022.

WEBSITES

Biology for Kids: Bacteria
www.ducksters.com/science/bacteria.php
Learn much more about bacteria at this detailed website.

Microbiology
www.amnh.org/explore/ology/microbiology
This exciting website include numerous videos, games, and activities related to the science of microbiology.

What Are Germs?
kidshealth.org/en/kids/germs.html
Find out more about bacteria and other organisms that cause illnesses.

Publisher's note to educators and parents: Our editors have carefully reviewed these websites to ensure that they are suitable for students. Many websites change frequently, however, and we cannot guarantee that a site's future contents will continue to meet our high standards of quality and educational value. Be advised that students should be closely supervised whenever they access the internet.

INDEX

A
antibiotics, 11, 16

C
cholera, 18, 19
colony, 6
cyanobacteria, 6, 7

E
Escherichia coli, 14, 15, 16

F
fossils, 7
food poisoning, 11, 14, 15, 16

L
Leeuwenhoek, Antonie van, 8, 9

M
microbiology, 8, 9
microscope, 4, 8
Middle Ages, 12

O
oxygen, 6

P
pandemic, 12, 13, 19
plague, 12, 14, 16

S
Salmonella, 8, 11, 14
Snow, John, 19

T
tetanus, 20
tuberculosis, 16, 17

V
vaccines, 11, 20
Vibro cholerae, 18
virus, 4

Y
Yersinia pestis, 12, 13